PEOPLE YOU
SHOULD KNOW

CESAR CHAVEZ

Get to Know the Leader Who Won Rights for Workers

by Rebecca Langston-George

Consultant:
Marc Grossman
Spokesman
Cesar Chavez Foundation

CAPSTONE PRESS
a capstone imprint

Fact Finders Books are published by Capstone Press,
1710 Roe Crest Drive, North Mankato, Minnesota 56003
www.mycapstone.com

Library of Congress Cataloging-in-Publication Data
Library of Congress Cataloging-in-Publication data is available on
the Library of Congress website.

ISBN 978-1-5435-5522-6 (library binding)
ISBN 978-1-5435-5922-4 (paperback)
ISBN 978-1-5435-5534-9 (eBook PDF)

Editorial Credits
Mari Bolte, editor; Kayla Rossow, designer; Svetlana Zhurkin, media researcher;
Tori Abraham, production specialist

Photo Credits
AP Photo, 21; Getty Images: Bettmann, 18, 27, Cathy Murphy, 14, Hulton Archive/Bob Parent,
25, NY Daily News Archive/Frank Hurley, cover; Library of Congress, 8, 11; Newscom: Everett
Collection, 23, Zuma Press/Mark Richards, 28; Shutterstock: Elena_Titova, 15; Walter P.
Reuther Library, Archives of Labor and Urban Affairs, Wayne State University, 5, 7, 12, 17; XNR
Productions, 20
Design Elements by Shutterstock

Source Notes
p. 21, line 13: "Happy Birthday Dolores Huerta." United Farm Workers. https://ufw.org/Happy-Birthday-
Dolores-Huerta/. Accessed 10 September 2018.

Printed in the United States of America.
PA48

TABLE OF CONTENTS

THE "NO" THAT PLANTED THE SEED

On his 35th birthday, Cesar Chavez quit the best-paying—and only steady—job he had ever had.

Cesar was the national staff director of the Community Service Organization (CSO). The CSO fought **discrimination** and worked to register voters. But as a former **migrant worker**, Cesar knew the nation's poorest workers needed help too. Cesar asked CSO to let him organize farm workers into a labor **union**.

Cesar was a talented organizer. He had built CSO into the most effective Latino **civil rights** group of its time. Even so, his idea was voted down. With that "no," Cesar decided that organizing farm workers would be his mission.

Cesar and his wife, Helen (right), with six of their eight children in 1969.

discrimination—treating people unfairly because of their identity, such as their race, country of birth, gender, or sexual orientation

migrant worker—a person who travels from place to place, looking for work

union—an organized group of workers set up to help improve such things as working conditions, wages, and health benefits

civil rights—the rights that all people have to freedom and equal treatment under the law

5

THE GREAT DEPRESSION

Cesar's grandfather Cesario left Mexico in the early 1880s. He settled in what was then the Arizona Territory, near Yuma. There, close to both the California and Mexico borders, he began to farm. Cesar's parents, Librado and Juana, also farmed the land and ran a small country store. Cesario ("Cesar") Estrada Chavez was born there on March 31, 1927. The family lived in the North Gila River Valley until Cesar was 11.

Young Cesar began his chores before the hot desert sun crept over the horizon. He fed the animals, chopped firewood, and gathered eggs before school. He also hunted rabbits and played on a small hill next to his house. Like many homes at the time, there was no electricity or indoor plumbing. Cesar and his younger brother, Richard, collected water from the canal for cooking, drinking, bathing, and washing clothes.

Even though the work was hard, the Chavez family loved their farm. Some two hundred aunts, uncles, and cousins lived nearby. They visited often and told stories around bonfires. Cesar and his brother swam and splashed in the canal and ate homegrown watermelon and corn.

the remains of Cesar's childhood home

But life changed during the Great Depression (1929–1939). Librado lost the store and couldn't pay taxes on the farm. The bank sold their farm when Cesar was 11. The family moved to California hoping for a fresh start.

The Great Depression's worst years were in the early 1930s. Around 13 million people were unemployed across the United States.

Hundreds of thousands of **bankrupt** families just like the Chavezes flooded California, desperate for work. Men called labor contractors promised good jobs with high wages and nice places to live. But in reality, most offered broken-down shacks, no bathrooms, and no rest breaks. Mexican Americans were paid less than white workers and often less than had been promised. Sometimes they even had to pay the contractor for water to drink.

The Great Depression

The **stock market** crash of the 1920s, along with a **drought** in the early 1930s, created the Great Depression and the Dust Bowl. Years of little rain caused dust storms in Oklahoma and other Midwestern states. With no crops to sell, farmers couldn't pay back bank loans and were forced to move. Like the Chavez family, more than 300,000 people came to California seeking farm work.

bankrupt—unable to pay debts

stock market—a place where stocks are bought and sold

drought—a long period of weather with little or no rainfall

The Chavez family moved from farm to farm. They lived in their car, a tent, or under bridges and trees. Cesar kept a little ball with him wherever they moved so he could play handball against the side of a building.

The entire family worked in the fields. However, Juana insisted her children go to school whenever possible. Cesar didn't like school. Teachers punished Cesar and his classmates for speaking Spanish. Because they moved so often, Cesar attended many different schools before dropping out after eighth grade.

Cesar worked in the fields full time to help his parents, often using the backbreaking short-handled hoe.

He joined the U.S. Navy in 1946 at the age of 19. Cesar never forgot the unfair treatment his family received as migrant farm workers. He thought by joining the Navy he could put it behind him. He was wrong.

The Devil's Arm

Growers often demanded their laborers use a hoe with a short handle. Farm workers called the 2-foot- (61-cm-) long hoe the "devil's arm." Hoes with long handles worked just as well and caused less back pain. But growers thought workers did a better job stooped over using the short-handled hoe.

Working 10 to 12 hours a day while bent over was damaging to the body. Children were especially vulnerable to permanent back pain after using the devil's arm.

DID YOU KNOW

Cesar met his wife, Helen, while they were both working in the fields around Delano, California. They married after he left the Navy.

CSO members in the 1950s. Cesar is second from the right in the first row. Fred Ross is in the middle. Helen Chavez is third from the right in the back row.

In 1952 Community Service Organization organizer Fred Ross knocked on Cesar's front door. Ross was organizing a chapter of the CSO, a civil rights group for Latino Americans. Their concerns were voter registration, immigration, resisting discrimination, and police brutality. Cesar wasn't interested. Finally, Cesar invited Ross into his home. He and his friends planned to pretend to listen. Then they would insult Ross until he left.

But nobody was insulted that night. Ross was persuasive. Hearing him speak began Cesar's career as a fighter for human rights.

Cesar worked with the CSO for a decade. As a community organizer he spoke to Latino Americans, including farm workers, around California. He listened to their problems and organized them to help themselves and receive the services they needed. He also encouraged them to become U.S. citizens, register to vote—and go out and vote. In 1959 he was named CSO national staff director.

But Cesar's request to organize farm workers was shot down by CSO in 1962. He decided he would start a union himself. The skills he learned at CSO would come in handy.

DID YOU KNOW

Cesar, Helen, and their eight children—Fernando, Sylvia, Linda, Elouise, Anna, Paul, Elizabeth, and Anthony—were the very first members of Cesar's new union.

First, Cesar and his family went on their annual one-week paid vacation—their last one. They pitched a tent on the beach. Cesar had saved $1,200. That money would help him travel around the state to build his union.

Though Helen and Cesar were willing to sacrifice for the cause, they had their eight children to think about. They moved to Delano, California, to be closer to their extended families. In the state's agricultural heartland, Delano would offer both jobs and access to future union members.

While Cesar traveled, Helen returned to work in the fields. She picked grapes and peas for 85 cents an hour. She rose before dawn to cook for her children. Then she put in 10 hours a day in the fields. When school was out, their older children worked in the fields too. Cesar joined them on weekends.

Helen played a huge role in Cesar's success. She did field work and raised their eight children so Cesar could organize. Later, she worked full time for the union.

Cesar traveled to farming towns up and down the great Central Valley. He met with farm workers where they lived. He knew workers wouldn't feel safe talking about a union at their jobs in the fields. Past attempts to organize had been shut down with violence and threats from growers. He needed workers to open their homes for meetings—just as Cesar had done for Fred Ross 10 years before.

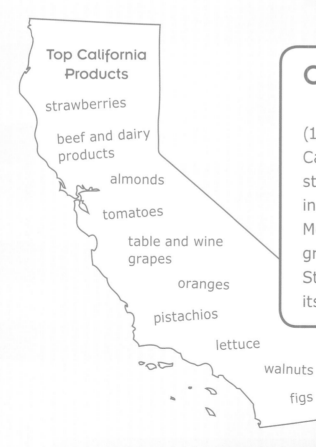

Top California Products

strawberries

beef and dairy products

almonds

tomatoes

table and wine grapes

oranges

pistachios

lettuce

walnuts

figs

California Agriculture

More than 43 million acres (17.4 million hectares) of land in California is used for farming. The state grows more than $46 billion in agricultural products every year. More than 400 different crops are grown there. One-third of the United States' vegetables and two-thirds of its fruits and nuts are grown there.

3 ▷ VIVA LA CAUSA!

Cesar met other organizers while he was with CSO, including Dolores Huerta and Gilbert Padilla. They started the work of organizing the National Farm Workers Association (NFWA). Its mission was to fight for fair wages and safe working conditions for agricultural workers.

The NFWA—which later would be called United Farm Workers (UFW)—had its founding convention on September 30, 1962. For $3.50 a month in union dues, the NFWA offered workers much-needed services. They promised to build a union that would fight for workers' rights. The NFWA flag was revealed. Its Aztec-style black eagle was designed by Cesar's brother Richard. The new union motto was "Viva La Causa"—long live the cause.

Dolores Huerta and Si, Se Puede

Dolores Fernandez Huerta (1930-) was a former teacher. She wanted to help her poor, hungry students. But she knew she had to improve their home life first.

Dolores and Cesar worked together organizing strikes and negotiating union contracts. The contracts improved pay, provided benefits, and eliminated hazardous working conditions. She is credited with creating the UFW's well-known slogan. After being told, "No, we can't!" many times during a meeting, Dolores shouted the new slogan: "Si, se puede!" ("Yes, we can!")

Dolores was jailed more than 20 times in her lifetime for protesting. At the age of 58 she was badly beaten by police. Her spleen was ruptured and she had four broken ribs. Though seriously injured, she continued to fight against racial and gender discrimination after her recovery. In 2012 she was awarded the Presidential Medal of Freedom by President Barack Obama.

Dolores Huerta (second from left) and Cesar (far right) at the first National Farm Workers Association convention in 1962

On September 8, 1965, Filipino grape workers around Delano went on strike. They were protesting low wages and long hours. The Filipinos asked Cesar's mostly Latino union to join their strike.

Cesar knew all farm workers had to work together. Race and language had intially separated them. But they learned that they had one thing in common: The need for a union to improve pay and conditions. If Cesar's members became **scabs** by working in the vineyards, it would weaken the Filipino workers' cause. A vote was held on September 16, 1965. All the NFWA members voted to join the Filipino grape workers' strike. They also took a pledge of nonviolence.

Picketers urged grape workers to strike. "Huelga" means "strike" in Spanish.

Every day, workers **picketed** at the vineyards. Growers attacked them with tractor dust, diesel exhaust, chemicals, and liquid fertilizer. They were beaten, threatened, and jailed despite their peaceful protests.

Workers who didn't strike still helped the cause. They slowed down the picking and packing process. Cesar welcomed college students who joined the picket lines. Some donated their lunch money on campus to the strikers. Religious and union leaders joined the cause, bringing money and food.

Strike

Strikes happen when workers stop working to make a protest. They hope to persuade their employer to change pay and working conditions. Striking workers often march in public places outside or near their job site. Signs and chants let other people know why they are striking. With no work being done, employers can't produce goods or services and they lose money.

scab—someone who takes the job of a union worker who is on strike
picket—to gather together in protest against a business

Sacramento ★
99
Lodi
Stockton · Manteca
Oakland · Modesto
Turlock
San Jose · Livingston · Merced
99 · Chowchilla
Madera · Highway City
Fresno · Parlier
Malaga · Cutler
Visalia · Farmersville
· Lindsay
99 · Porterville
Delano · Ducor
65
Bakersfield
99 · Arvin
Oxnard
Los Angeles

California

Nevada

Pacific
Ocean

Route of the march

N
W · E
S

0   50 miles
0   50 kilometers

After six months, union leaders came
up with a plan. They would focus national
attention on the strike. On March 17, 1966,
Cesar led strikers on a march stretching more
than 300 miles (483 km). They walked from
Delano to Sacramento, California, shouting,
"Viva La Causa!" Farm workers in every town
along the route joined the march. They also
cheered them on, fed them, and housed them.

Near the end of the march, Cesar received a message. Schenley Industries, one company the union was striking, wanted to settle. Cesar drove to Beverly Hills to meet with a company attorney. Cesar and the Schenley workers signed a union contract, giving the workers a raise.

The march continued. The marchers arrived, feet blistered and bloody, in Sacramento on Easter Sunday. Dolores stood in front of news cameras. She presented the farm workers' demands to the governor and legislators. She wanted workers to have the power to improve their wages and working conditions. "You cannot close your eyes and ears to us any longer," she said.

Cesar's march ended on April 10, 1966, on the steps of the California State Capitol.

THE NONVIOLENT STRUGGLE

The Schenley victory lifted the workers' spirits, but most growers wouldn't budge. The Delano grape strike would last five years. The union needed a new plan.

Cesar decided to start a grape **boycott**. If consumers didn't buy grapes and growers lost money, they'd meet strikers' demands. Grape strikers and their families fanned out across the United States and Canada. They told their stories and spread the word about the boycott. Soon, people across North America wouldn't buy grapes. Some transportation unions joined the fight. They refused to deliver grapes.

Peaceful Protests

Cesar and the UFW followed the teachings of Mahatma Gandhi and Martin Luther King Jr. (MLK.) In the 1930s Gandhi campaigned for India's independence from Great Britain. He organized a salt boycott to protest Britain's taxes on salt. He led a march across India. He was also known for going on fasts as part of his nonviolent struggle.

MLK was a civil rights leader also known for marching and peaceful protests. During Cesar's fast, he sent Cesar a telegram praising him for his work.

boycott—to refuse to take part in or buy something as a way of making a protest

fast—to give up eating for a period of time for moral or religious reasons

Although the strike and boycott were starting to gain ground, some union members were impatient. They didn't like the slow progress and daily harassment by the growers. They lost faith in Cesar's ideas. They damaged some equipment in frustration. So Cesar stopped eating. He **fasted** for 25 days. He hoped fasting would show his personal commitment to nonviolence. He lost 35 pounds, but the people listened.

Senator Robert Kennedy helped Cesar break his fast on March 10, 1968.

5 ▷ THE SALAD BOWL STRIKE

With support from millions of consumers, the grape boycott affected growers' profits. Eventually they gave in. By 1970 growers and the UFW signed contracts. They recognized the union and raised wages. That ended the grape strike and boycott.

Cesar's work wasn't done. Less than a month later, he took on lettuce and vegetable growers. The targeted farms were in the Salinas Valley and along the coast of central California. It was the largest agricultural strike in history. The demands were the same: Better pay, benefits, and a union of their own to fight for their rights. About 10,000 lettuce and vegetable workers went on strike. A **rural** judge ordered Cesar to stop the boycott. He refused, and was jailed for 20 days in December 1970. But the boycott worked.

In 1973 Coretta Scott King (second from left) joined Cesar (center) to boycott lettuce in New York City.

Five more years of strikes and boycotts followed. Strikers convinced lawmakers to pass the state Agricultural Labor Relations Act of 1975. It gave California farm workers more rights. They could freely assemble, organize, and negotiate union contracts with their employers.

DID YOU KNOW?

Crops such as grapes and lettuce need a lot of skilled farm workers to grow and pick them. Once they are ripe, these crops will rot quickly if they are not harvested. Because of this, they were ideal for striking.

rural—having to do with the countryside or farming

25

A MONUMENT IN HIS HONOR

In the summer of 1975, Cesar led a 1,000-mile (1,609-km) march up and down California. Farm workers had new rights thanks to the state farm labor law. Cesar wanted everyone to know about those rights. The march took him 58 days. Thousands of workers joined the march. They showed up at evening rallies to hear Cesar speak and get organized.

In April 1975 the state of California banned the short-handled hoe. At his father's funeral in 1982, Cesar laid a hoe on top of his casket. The farm worker movement donated another hoe to the National Museum of American History. Workers could finally stand tall.

In the mid-1980s, enforcement of the farm labor law ended. Cesar renewed his grape boycott. The renewed boycott also demanded an end to the use of harmful **pesticides**. They were poisoning workers and their children. They also threatened the health of consumers. Cesar fasted for 36 days in 1988 to spread awareness. Celebrities joined him in fasting.

Cesar fought to ban four harmful chemicals used by California grape growers.

pesticide—poisonous chemical used to kill insects, rats, and fungi that can damage plants

After 31 years of striking, boycotting, fasting, marching, and protesting, Cesar Chavez finally rested. He died in Arizona on April 23, 1993, just a short distance away from his birthplace. He spent his last day defending the union in court against a large vegetable grower. Some 50,000 people attended his funeral. He was buried at his movement's 187-acre (75.7-hectare) headquarters in Keene, California, near Bakersfield.

Cesar in 1990

In 1994 President Bill Clinton presented the Presidential Medal of Freedom to Helen Chavez. She accepted it for her late husband. His picture was put on a postage stamp in 2003. His birthday, March 31, is now a holiday in 11 states. The U.S. Navy named its latest dry cargo ship USNS *Cesar Chavez*. Thousands of communities hold events each year honoring Cesar. Hundreds of public places have been named for him. Many school and community groups hold a day of service around his birthday. They clean up trash or graffiti or feed the homeless. Although he is gone, his legacy lives on.

His Final Resting Place

In 2012 President Barack Obama dedicated the Cesar E. Chavez National Monument, the 398th unit of the National Park Service. The monument stands in the small town of Keene, California, where Cesar lived and worked his last quarter century. The Visitor Center has exhibits on UFW history. Cesar's office is visible through a window, with his Presidential Medal of Freedom on display. Cesar and Helen's graves are side by side nearby. They are inside the walls of the beautifully landscaped Memorial Garden.

GLOSSARY

bankrupt (BANK-rupht)—unable to pay debts

boycott (BOY-kot)—to refuse to take part in or buy something as a way of making a protest

civil rights (SI-vil RYTS)—the rights that all people have to freedom and equal treatment under the law

discrimination (dis-kri-muh-NAY-shuhn)—treating people unfairly because of their identity, such as their race, country of birth, gender, or sexual orientation

drought (DROUT)—a long period of weather with little or no rainfall

fast (FAST)—to give up eating for a period of time for moral or religious reasons

migrant worker (MYE-gruhnt WURK-uhr)—a person who travels from place to place, looking for work

pesticide (PES-tuh-side)—poisonous chemical used to kill insects, rats, and fungi that can damage plants

picket (PIK-it)—to gather together in protest against a business

rural (RUR-uhl)—having to do with the countryside or farming

scab (SKAB)—someone who takes the job of a union worker who is on strike

stock market (STOCK MAHR-kit)—a place where stocks are bought and sold; someone who owns a stock owns part of a company

union (YOON-yuhn)—an organized group of workers set up to help improve such things as working conditions, wages, and health benefits

READ MORE

Brill, Marlene Targ. *Dolores Huerta Stands Strong: The Woman Who Demanded Justice*. Biographies for Young Readers. Athens, Ohio: Ohio University Press, 2018.

Rau, Dana Meachen. *Who Was Cesar Chavez?* Who Was . . . New York: Grosset & Dunlap, an imprint of Penguin Random House, 2017.

Yasuda, Anita. *Children Working the Fields*. Mendota Heights, Minn.: Focus Readers, 2018.

INTERNET SITES

Use FactHound to find Internet sites related to this book.

Visit *www.facthound.com*

Just type in 9781543555226 and go.

Check out projects, games and lots more at
www.capstonekids.com

CRITICAL THINKING QUESTIONS

1. Using evidence from the text and other sources, list the ways the labor of farm workers is undervalued.

2. Do you think a boycott is an effective technique to pressure a company to make changes? Why or why not?

3. As part of the Cesar Chavez holiday, many people honor Cesar's memory by taking part in a day of service in their community. Write a paragraph describing how you'd serve your community for a day in Cesar's honor.

INDEX